Martin Fiedler

Bible 21

The Sense of Life

How Facts Outshine Faith and Prove the
Reality of Jesus Christ

© 2021 Martin Fiedler

Publishing & Printing:
tredition GmbH, Halenreie 40-44, 22359 Hamburg, Germany

ISBN:

978-3-347-40267-6	(Paperback)
978-3-347-40268-3	(Hardcover)
978-3-347-40269-0	(e-Book)

Bibliographic information of the German National Library: The German National Library lists this publication in the German National Bibliography; detailed bibliographic data are available on the Internet at http://dnb.d-nb.de

Content

Preface

As a little boy I used to lie in the grass at night and look at the stars in the night sky and ask myself again and again why I exist – why we exist and what sense life has on earth at all. And I was also fascinated by the fact that life as such only exists because an extremely large number of constellations had to fit together so that life could arise in this quality at all.

These many constellations, like the formation of atmosphere, water, distance sun to earth etc. are even more incredible, because the alternative to these "MEGA-many" coincidences, would have been "NOTHING".

Two things have been drivers of my thoughts in my life since then because of this:

1. Behind these incredibly many prerequisites, which were necessary in view of the emergence of life and mankind, there must inevitably be a perfect mathematical blueprint – the most beautiful and magical blueprint that outshines everything that human architecture in all its facets has ever produced.

2. The alternative "NOTHING" means no existence – no life or other matter at all. But since the universe, the earth and life are reality and ultimately EVERYTHING is based on mathematical-physical and chemical laws, the following two facts result from this:

  1. First-Fact: From NOTHING nothing can come into being!

  2. Second-Fact: Deriving from the mathematical-physical and chemical regularities elementary for our existence, as well as connected with the 1st fact – from NOTHING nothing can come into being – inevitably an unbelievable and powerful creative intelligence unimaginable for humans must underlie EVERYTHING.

And in this intelligence, I see not only a mathematical-physical-chemical intelligence, but also a coalescing, supernatural intelligence – multifaceted and complex – which at the same time seems to reveal the beauty for the development and unfolding of human souls.

In this context, the often unpleasant or even tragic experiences in our lives may seem partly incomprehensible to us humans from the present perspective. However, the unpleasant and painful experiences in our lives seem to be indispensable as a necessary part for our soul development. More about this in Chapter 2 – Messages about the sense of existence.

Nevertheless, I personally see the blueprint of the world (and the universe) as perfect, because it is based on mathematical, physical and chemical laws that are comprehensible to us and these are simply pure facts – only humans themselves are the weakest link in the chain and often have to painfully experience and learn on the way to the expansion of the wisdom of the soul that they are the "imperfect" part in a "perfect" system that is only heading for one big goal:

The UNIFICATION of all life in a world not based on matter and the return to unconditional love.

1. Introduction

Within the introduction I would like to inform you on the one hand briefly about my person, on the other hand give a small overview of the further book contents.

What has happened since the little boy looked up at the starry sky and asked himself the question about the sense of life.

My personal development is based on the two original thoughts already mentioned, which I already had as a child. To write about a title component of this book "The Sense of Life" also only makes sense from my point of view, provided that you as the author were able to consciously and strategically bring your own intrinsic abilities into your life in every respect. In other words: the sense of life is, among other things, to discover one's own abilities and also to be able to live them out and bring them to fruition.

Originally, I had started to study architecture after my A level (Abitur), but since I couldn't draw freehand – we had to draw whole landscapes in maybe an hour – I decided relatively quickly to study business administration, which I also successfully completed in Mainz.

After my diploma thesis in retail, I started a retail career in sales and am up to now still enthusiastically responsible for the development of managers in senior sales management.

Just as the universe is subject to a grand architectural plan, it is also necessary – in order to be able to lead a successful and thus meaningful life – to develop one's own life architecture based on one's own intrinsic motives.

My "life architecture" is based on findings that I have been able to publish in three books so far with the publishing house Springer Gabler.
The first book entitled "Guide to Success", (1st edition 2012 under the title "Personality and Success") was published as 3rd edition in 2020.

In "Guide to Success," universal laws for life success are brought closer to the reader within an easy-to-understand story.

These laws have supported me, among other things, to keep my personal development, satisfaction and thus happiness in balance and thus ultimately to be personally successful, because success is linked to one's own satisfaction.

Essentially, it is about finding your own tasks in life for which you feel love, enthusiasm and dedication. Then you will probably always be better than the average in what you do and thus ultimately mostly earn more money than the average as a waste product of your work. He who loves expands his mind, which can expand and one opens, so to speak, the gate into a wonderful world. Thus, one can satisfy one's often latent needs for self-realization.

And always try to approach things positively – a smile costs nothing – but may make others happy. What you radiate comes back to you and with it you can even satisfy your own appreciation needs.

And have respect for others and respect others. Pay attention to their self-esteem, so even if you have different opinions, you will be able to have successful conversations with everyone. This also satisfies one's social needs for successful communication with others.

You see, respect for these laws brings satisfaction of needs and thus happiness. In any case, I would regard this state as a personal success, because the consideration of the universal laws described by me creates simultaneously satisfaction directed INWARD-LY and OUTWARDLY and thus fulfilment. This is meaningful or not?

The most valuable things in life cannot be bought: personal success, which is linked to inner satisfaction, love and enthusiasm for tasks and purpose in life, appreciation by others, friends, health, to name but a few.

It should also be mentioned that one should distance oneself from any negative emotions, such as envy or ill-will, etc., and replace them by always being sincerely happy for others and their success – which means that one should always practice positive action without exception.

These regularities have also helped me greatly in my leadership roles and in the development of my leaders.

As a leader, you can only be successful if you in turn can empower and develop the leaders for whom you are responsible.

I was able to publish my findings from personnel management in my 3rd book entitled "Successful Employee Management and Control in Retail Business". And I have also been able to empirically prove these findings. By applying and implementing the leadership principles I developed and refined, the best economic figures by far were demonstrably achieved in comparison. Thus, these findings represent a novelty in the field of the presentation of leadership principles in the professional literature.

And this content, in turn, I could only develop in this form, because I have always thought and acted on the basis of my upstream insights, which I described in the book "Guide to Success". So ultimately everything builds on each other.

I have always been able to use personal knowledge enhancement in a conscious and structured way.

Why am I telling you all this, you may ask?

Well, what I am writing about in the work "Bible 21 – The Sense of Life" – is something special – it is a big title. And the facts as well as circumstantial evidence of the reality of Jesus Christ are much bigger.

It is wonderful and magical at the same time. And it is, from my point of view, the biggest and most important topic in the world. And that is why it is important to me that you know that here is not some "crazy person" writing a book about the greatest thing of ALL TIME.

In addition, it is important for me to tell you about my personal development in life, in order to be able to understand why the idea arose in me to write this book.

Writing a book, by the way, already helps the author to channel his numerous experiences and thoughts and the language as such also serves to make many things even more transparent. In this respect, it can help every person in his or her personal development when thoughts are written down, even if it does not have to be a book for publication.
As soon as you write, energy will flow and this will help to see thoughts more clearly.

Our thinking shapes us, our personality and our character. And we have influence on our thinking. And it is interesting to think about our own thinking. Therefore, chapter 1 deals with how our thinking determines our life.

In chapter 2, I have summarized the most important messages of a medium about the sense of existence and with it the development and wisdom of our soul. With the information from these trance messages, however, no claim is made to sound scientific knowledge. This information is to be regarded as hypothetical. It is my opinion, however, that this concrete information is an enrichment for the whole context.

In chapter 3, I will touch on easily understandable facts, which we can deduce from the blueprint of the universe.

Chapter 4 will then follow with facts and circumstantial evidence of the Resurrection of Jesus Christ based on purely scientific research of the Shroud of Turin.

This book is not meant to simply point out facts that prove the Resurrection and thus the reality of Jesus Christ.

The sense of our life is elementary after all and is ultimately inseparable from the reality of Jesus Christ. In this respect, the title "Bible 21" and the "Sense of Life" is a work that presents the ultimate sense of life in connection with Jesus Christ from a different perspective to the traditional Bible. It is about the expansion of bundled knowledge that can replace faith.

Even back then when Jesus Christ stood bodily in front of people and practically gave direct evidence of the Resurrection, there were "doubters", even though they experienced it bodily. What must it be like for us people today who did not experience the whole thing? But there were also those who knew, and I personally consider this state of knowing to be the clearly better one.

Knowledge instead of faith is the only option for me as an analytically and logically thinking person. All the more fascinating are the scientific findings and the incredible sum of facts and circumstantial evidence that Jesus Christ and the Resurrection must be reality.

And it is precisely the Resurrection that is the all-important factor. For without the Resurrection the whole of Christianity would be worth nothing.

Mere facts do not always convince people. To just skim the surface of the beauty, clarity and perfection of the mathematical foundations of the universe and to be able to comprehend the power and evolution of our thoughts opens up a wonderful world and changes our own perspective and understanding of the world.

This book is for all people who want to know more about

   ... the sense of life

   ... personal success

   ... and the fascination of the reality of Jesus Christ.

I hope that this work can help us to understand that Jesus Christ is a reality and that faith has become practically superfluous.

2. Our thinking determines our life

"Watch your thoughts, for they become words; watch your words, for they become actions; watch your actions, for they become habits; watch your habits, for they become your character; watch your character, for it becomes your destiny" (by Charles Reade, 1814-1884)

Our thoughts alone are the origin of everything that arises and in them lies the key to a fulfilled life. We ourselves can determine what we think and thus decide how we perceive the world and where we personally develop.

If we think that our neighbour is an "idiot", then he is an "idiot", because we think that way and because this thinking is part of our worldview. And if we think that we had a difficult and unlovely childhood, it is because we think that way. If we think the rainy weather is bad, it is bad because everything is the way we think. But we also have the power over our thinking and we can also choose to think that our neighbour is okay, thus he is also okay because we think so. We can also think that our childhood was fine, then it was fine because we think so and we can also think that the rainy weather is nice and good for the plants, then it is so. That's how simple thinking works.

We alone create our world through our thinking. And thus, as many worlds exist as humans exist. We should handle this power consciously, respectfully and carefully. Because through our thinking our character is formed.

All actions result from our thoughts.

"When a man cherishes evil thoughts in his conscious-ness, pain comes upon him just as the wheel comes behind the ox. If a man cherishes pure thoughts, joy follows him like his own shadow – certainly." (James Allen).

Just as cause and effect are interrelated in the material and visible world, the same is true in the world of thought.

"A noble and godly character is not a thing of favour or accident, but the natural result of continual efforts at right thinking, the result of a long-cultivated alliance with godly thoughts. An unworthy and rude character is, by the same process, the result of perpetual cherishing of low thoughts." (James Allen)

"Man creates or forfeits himself. In the forge of thought he makes the weapons with which he destroys himself. He likewise makes the tools with which he builds for himself heavenly abodes of joy, power, and peace. If he chooses the right thoughts and uses them truly, man ascends to divine perfection. By misuse and wrong employment of thoughts he sinks below the level of the animal. Between these two extremes lie all degrees of characters, and man is their creator and master." (James Allen)

We should make a conscious effort every day to become a better person than we were the day before.

It always starts with the first thought for it. And in my opinion with continuous self-reflection.

And since I personally like to work with instructions – I prefer short instructions – I would like to offer again a thought framework as a basis for thought development so that it is easier to work with the really noble thoughts in practice:

1. Find out who you are, what talents and abilities you have. If you have difficulties with this, keep a diary and write down every day what you have done well. This will probably seem a bit strange at first. But if you look at your entries again after a few weeks, you can discover things that may have remained hidden from you before. There is a hidden genius in everyone. It is important to bring

this to the surface and from now on to promote these intrinsic aspects, to develop them and to bring them into your own life. The point is to live in harmony with one's own personality. This is the inwardly directed task, where one should direct one's thinking.

2. Practice positive outward action every day: smile and think of three things to look forward to in the morning.
   For example: a good lunch, meet a friend, play sports;
   Just be a sunshine in the truest sense of the word.

3. Be polite and respectful to all and sundry; respect the SSW (sense of self-worth) of your interlocutors and you will always have a continuing basis for conversation even if you have different opinions.

4. Throw all negative thoughts and emotions overboard.
   Henceforth, there must be no room in your life for:
   - Envy
   - Resentment
   - Hate
   - Deceit
   - etc.

Replace these negative thoughts with positive benevolent emotions. Be happy for others and their success. Be sincere in your thoughts and actions.

Whoever links his thinking to this framework of thoughts, reflects himself and pursues the goal of becoming a better person every day, will develop further personally.

And the personal striving for development is meaningful. A disoriented drifting does not create sustainable satisfaction and thus also no sustainable success or sense of happiness.

3. Messages about the sense of existence

"The soul of man is like water. From heaven it comes, to heaven it rises. And down again to the earth it must go. Eternally changing"... (J. W. von Goethe)

"Since we ate from the Tree of Knowledge, Paradise is locked and the Cherub is behind us. We must make the journey around the world and see if perhaps it is open again from behind somewhere." (H. von Kleist)

In this chapter, I try to summarize what I could learn about the sense of existence through the trance messages of a medium. This information is not scientific and should be considered hypothetical.

A medium has the ability to receive so-called announcements from the beyond. Varda Hasselmann and Frank Schmolke have presented this subject impressively and factually in the book "Wisdom of the Soul" – trance messages about the sense of existence.

Comparable to the developmental steps of the human being from the new-born to the child, adolescent, adult up to the elderly senior, the soul also has to pass through an incarnation cycle over many centuries and millennia. And this applies to all human beings without exception.

In this case, five soul cycles are presented:

- Infant Soul
- Child Soul
- Young Soul
- Mature Soul
- Old Soul

Each of these soul cycles thus comprises a further seven clearly defined stages – i.e., a total of 35 stages – with each stage being based on a clear task of development.

Each task of development can take one to four human lifetimes, and the next stage can only begin after the previous task of development has been completed.

There is no value between the stages. There is no value between a baby, a child, or an adult. Every human being usually goes through many stages of age. And as a man matures, so does the soul. But the soul needs many human lives, until it has gone through and completed all the tasks of development.

An affinity for this approach – according to the authors – is only reserved to "mature souls" of the third stage, who then also visit their seminar, in order to be able to experience, for example, quite concretely, which life task they are currently going through.

According to this, even the political form of society is determined by the composition of the degree of maturity of the souls. In the Federal Republic of Germany about fifty percent are Young Souls and just under thirty percent are Mature Souls.

"Young souls" of the first stages, tend to have fundamentalist attitudes. There are therefore no right or wrong ideas or fundamental attitudes. These are, as a rule, attitudes appropriate to the soul's age.

For example, if a four-year-old child believes in Santa Claus, then that is fine and we should not talk the child out of that idea either. With an adult, however, this idea would not be appropriate.

Therefore, there is no better or worse stage in the development of the soul. According to this approach, we humans go through all stages.

Once all stages have been passed through, according to the authors, the soul unites with its soul family, which usually consists of about 1000 individual souls.

And also in this area, the soul family must develop further in order to be able to reach higher layers. By the way, the medium Varda Hasselmann receives her messages from such a reunited soul family – she calls it the source which consists of the soul essences of sages and scholars – who gladly support and help to advance their own development.

The goal of the development and unfolding of the soul is described as a path back to love and the Whole Entire.

The Whole Entire can be understood in our imagination as a kind of layered model. This layering of different vibrational intensities and vibrational qualities of energy has more love and understanding the higher the vibrational level.

This hypothesis of the development of the soul over many human lives, by incarnating between 35 to over 100 times, is an approach that is definitely in the context of what constitutes the overall sense of life – namely the development of love in all facets – in order to be able to reverse the expulsion from paradise in the biblical sense, for a return to the WHOLE ENTIRE.

The fact that there is a lot of injustice and evil in the world and also unbelievably bad strokes of fate and suffering, as well as wars, etc., is, according to the medium, an irrevocable necessity for the development of the soul.

Incidentally, the medium can ask the source all conceivable questions – for example, inquire about the meaning of a war or a specific misfortune. The source answers them and for this reason a comprehensive structure and knowledge from this non-material world could be gathered in the meantime.

Some people may have turned away from Jesus Christ, because perhaps bad things have happened to them personally, or perhaps they can no longer reconcile the suffering in the world with faith in Jesus Christ.

However, we humans are the "imperfect" ones in a "perfect" world, and as I have already shown, we humans are the weakest link in the chain.

We are the shapers, we forge our destiny, we are the imperfect ones in a perfect world. We bring suffering upon ourselves. We were, in the biblical sense, the ones who ate from the forbidden fruit and were therefore driven out of paradise.

Thus, it is just suitable for us human beings to reject responsibility and to place ourselves comfortably in the role of victims and, as the forgers of our humble destiny, to push faith in Jesus Christ far away from us.

We are the ones who should not complain, but give honor to our spiritual possibilities in comparison to the animal world and shape this wonderful life with full gratitude.

Instead, we use only a fraction of our mental faculties.

If you do not understand or cannot comprehend, or if you judge too quickly, you should first use your mind and change your perspective. And I do that by being open to a change of perspective, despite my analytical and rational disposition.

For this reason, I see the information in this chapter as an adequate piece of the mosaic in the overall context.

4. Knowledge instead of belief

Besides the holy scriptures, the Word of God is embodied in all the real laws of the universe.

The world we live in and we ourselves, if we disregard the theory of chances, were created by our Creator.

It therefore makes sense to deal with the laws of this real world and of the universe, because they are therefore the real laws of God.

Insofar as we violate scientific laws, natural laws will be our judges and we our own executioners. For example, it is our choice to eat a poisonous mushroom or not – we have the choice, whereas ignorance or stupidity does not protect us from punishment.

There are different theories about the origin of the universe. However, it is assumed that highly compressed mass began to expand abruptly in a gigantic explosion – the big bang theory. According to this theory, the universe continues to expand infinitely.

There are other theories that say that the universe expands to a certain point and then contracts again, ending back in a highly compressed mass.

Gravity is the force in the universe that holds planets and suns together. Larger masses attract smaller masses, like the sun attracts the earth, whereby its orbital speed becomes smaller. After this process, in a few billion years, the sun will absorb the earth.

The basic structure of the universe is made up of the smallest particles (including electrons, neutrons, protons, neutrinos, muons, baryons, quarks). Many gigantic galaxy systems have developed from this. All this is based on physical laws and therefore there must be an intelligence underlying everything, which already existed before the big bang.

And all built up matter is a kind of life. Because everything possesses a certain form of intelligence and is therefore also expression of a kind of life form.

Intelligence is defined, among other things, as perceptiveness, cleverness, knowledge, etc.

Thus, not only humans possess intelligence, but also animals or plants.

Plants, for example, orient their leaves according to the sun, which requires some form of perceptiveness and/or knowledge. This is stored knowledge.

Matter attracts matter to unite. For example, gravitational energy causes a coconut to fall to earth. The larger mass attracts the smaller mass. This can also be seen as a kind of perception and thus intelligence.

Both masses, the earth as well as the coconut determine in each case that an attraction (gravity) is emitted and cause them to move towards the other body respectively. The matters know in which direction they are heading and who is moving towards whom. The result is that matter possesses a communication system and thus ultimately the entire universe.

Until today, gravity can be measured, but its origin cannot be explained.

Ultimately, all matter has a creative structure and everything is subject to mathematical-physical and chemical laws. Everything has structure in the large as well as in the small matter and the large matter is built up from the small matter.

Now, one can hypothesize that either all structure is subject to chance or the structure was created by a higher intelligence.

My view: Since everything creative is subject to clear, unambiguous, comprehensible and logical laws and structures, and since these laws and structures have so far not been able to provide us with a single example of something coming into being out of NOTHING, there must inevitably be a creative force underlying EVERY-THING, which also has a clear idea and blueprint for the realization of a great goal.

And this goal of unification and return to the WHOLE ENTIRE or return to paradise or unification in a non-material world in connection with the development of our soul and love, does not seem to be unrealistic when looking at different levels in this book.

Because both the aspects of our thinking, as well as the information about the developmental steps of our soul and the consideration of what we have been able to experience about our world and the universe, result in a harmonious overall picture. Each area is like a mosaic stone and all areas together give a picture of a wonderful and supernatural loving power.

5. Facts about the Resurrection

Superimposed on this overall picture is the world's most extensive scientific knowledge of a man's shroud, from which his Resurrection can be deduced.

This scientifically most extensively examined object in the world in more than 500,000 hours has yielded a result that seems to prove the unbelievable phenomenon of a Resurrection.

This Resurrection is consistent in incredible detail with the biblical accounts of the Resurrection of Jesus Christ. It is the Shroud of Turin.

The Shroud of Turin very probably shows the body and face of Jesus Christ, which was transferred from the body to the cloth at the moment of the Resurrection by a complex physical phenomenon.

In the many centuries until today, the shroud had to be rescued from fire several times. In the process, individual parts had to be repaired and replaced. A test from 1988, which dated the shroud to the Middle Ages, was demonstrably made with such a corner piece of the shroud, which was subsequently added to the shroud at that time for repair and restoration.

This piece used for restoration is made of cotton, while the intact part of the cloth is made of linen. Linen is significantly more durable and stable than cotton, as the flax fibre itself is extremely tear-resistant. As a result, products made from linen are exceptionally durable. Cotton products wear out more and more over the years.

Using the radiocarbon method, it had already been analysed in 1982 that this shroud must date from the year 30 to 70. The shroud has a length of 440 cm and a width of 110 cm. The height of the man depicted on the shroud is 180 cm.

Men in the first century were on average 165 cm tall and thus on average 15 cm shorter.

The fabric of the shroud is of very high quality, which therefore only rich people could afford.

This agrees with reports from the Bible. There we are told about the rich disciple Joseph from Arimathea (Mathew 27,57,58) ...*But in the evening came a rich man of Arimathea, whose name was Joseph, who was also a disciple of Jesus. He went to Pilate and asked him for the body of Jesus. Then Pilate commanded that it should be given to him....*

In the embalming of the body, over a dozen herbs and pollen were used, the traces of which were analysed in the shroud and which grow exclusively near Jerusalem in Israel and have been dated to the time of Jesus Christ.

Analysed dirt at the foot of the shroud was assigned to the area around the Damascus Gate in Jerusalem.

Coins were placed on the eyes, the image of which was also transferred to the shroud and have an imprint of Emperor Tiberius. These date from the period 29 to 32 of the first century.

The examinations and analyses clearly showed that the shroud depicts a crucified man with wounds on his hands and feet. The thumbs are bent inwards in a cramped manner, which shows that the nails, which were driven through the wrists, have penetrated the nerve tracts.

The analyses also revealed that the man had been stabbed in the side of the torso with a pointed object. This agrees with the report from the Bible (John 19,34) *... one of the soldiers thrust his lance into his side, and immediately blood flowed out...*

In addition, an incredible number of traces of torture with 120 wounds have been analysed. These result from lashes with a Roman whip, which was equipped with 3 lead balls. In total, 270 wounds are visible and can be extrapolated to around 600 wounds, since the shroud depicts the front and back, but not the sides of the body.

Investigations also revealed that two men of different sizes carried out the torture, one being a left-handed man.

The traces of the crown of thorns, which are visible with 30 punctures on the head, were also analysed.

The blood residue analyses of type AB on the shroud revealed high levels of creatinine and ferritin, which are commonly found in the blood of those who have been violently killed.
The man in the shroud undoubtedly suffered a very gruesome death. The variously analysed blood remains clearly show both blood remains of a dead person and blood which proves that the person was previously alive. The reason for this is that even during the scourging while still alive, blood came from the wounds onto the skin and was subsequently transferred to the cloth, and likewise blood was transferred to the cloth after death had occurred, for example, through the discharge of blood onto the skin immediately after the lance thrust, at which time Jesus Christ was already dead.

There are no signs of decomposition, suggesting that the man was wrapped in the cloth for a maximum of 48 hours after his death.

The blood on the cloth remained curiously red, although it should normally turn dark through oxidation. The blood was also already on the cloth before the image was formed in the cloth. The image of the man was not transferred under the blood stains.

Letters in Aramaic, Latin and Greek were also discovered on the shroud and analysed by Barbara Frale. These letters were used to mark the body of the deceased. Papyrus strips with large letters placed on the head clearly show the name "Yahushua Nnazarennos" – Jesus of Nazareth, as well as other information that, according to analyses, dates from the 1st century.

In 2006, the analysis of the face print on the shroud revealed three Hebrew letters that became visible through ultraviolet and infrared light. The letters form the Hebrew word for "lamb", which is used in the second book of Moses and refers to Jesus Christ as the Passover lamb (1st Corinthians 5,7).

The image on the shroud is extremely thin, only 0.007 millimetres, which corresponds to 7 micrometres. For several years, attempts were made to reproduce the image on linen.

High-tech lasers that emit short bursts of ultraviolet light were used for this purpose. This has made it technically possible to achieve a rough approximation of the texture of the image on the shroud, at least on a few square centimetres. However, even with the technology available today, it has never been possible to produce a complete authentic duplicate.

The experimental physicist Paolo Di Lazzaro says the ultraviolet light needed to create the image must be stronger than any ultraviolet light source available around the world today.

To produce such an image, shocks shorter than 40 billionths of a second and with a power of several billion watts were required. The beam of light must be no wider than one hundredth of a human hair, since only one of 200 fibres of the linen fabric on the shroud was hit by the light.

Only the so-called UV-B – Dorno radiation of ultraviolet light – fulfilled these requirements. This source of light must have been of unimaginable magnitude (1st Timothy 6,16) that through it even an image of the bones and 23 teeth became visible in an analysis by x-ray imaging and were ultimately also transferred to the cloth.

This proves that no legs and bones were broken, which was completely untypical for a crucifixion at that time, because they wanted to prevent the crucified from pushing himself up with his legs to be able to breathe better. (John 19, 32-33) ...*Then the soldiers came and broke the legs of the first one and also of the other who was crucified with him. But when they came to Jesus and saw that he was already dead, they did not break his legs; but one of the soldiers pierced his side with a lance....*

The particle physicist Isabel Piczek believes that the moment of Resurrection was accompanied by two event horizons, where the laws of physics and space-time are changed. An event horizon cuts space-time in half, so to speak, so that space and time are stopped for a very small moment.

The physicist further states that the event horizons were caused in the centre of the body and forces under and above the body caused the shroud to tighten and quantum time to collapse to zero. This dissolved gravity and the body must have floated parallel to the shroud, explaining why no couch marks, deformed muscles, etc. were transferred to the shroud and image.

Only in this way could the real proportions of the front and back of the body at the moment of the Resurrection be transferred upwards and downwards as an image.

According to the presentation of the physicist Mrs. Isabel Piczek, the process of Resurrection can be described as a kind of big bang – scientists call this a singularity – in which an infinitely small point that stood at the beginning of creation and triggered the beginning of its creation and expansion through the big bang.

This event caused an earthquake at that time (Matthew 28,2) ... *And behold, there was a great earthquake. Because an angel of the Lord came down from heaven, and stood by, and rolled away the stone...* and there took place in the tomb of Jesus Christ a process which may be called the start of a new creation. (2nd Corinthians 5,17) ... *Therefore, if any man be in Christ, he is a new creature: old things have passed away; behold, new things have come into being.*

The numerous facts and circumstantial evidence concerning the Shroud of Turin clearly suggest that the Resurrection and therefore Jesus Christ is a reality, and the Shroud bears the negative image of Jesus Christ – created at the moment of the Resurrection.

Concluding remarks

The realization of the reality of Jesus Christ seems intangible and magical at the same time. My thoughts keep seeing this miracle and at the same time I think about how I can and should develop personally.

Every path begins with the first step

... and the way back to paradise
... back to the Whole Entire
... back to unconditional love

...begins with right and noble thinking.

Even though this book allows you to perceive all the pieces of the mosaic as one overall picture, you look at infinity in amazement.

Jesus Christ is the only thing that remains.

Honour him.

Literature

James Allen. 2017. As a man thinks, so does he live. Munich: mvgverlag

Varda Hasselmann and Frank Schmolke. 1995. Wisdom of the Soul, Trance Messages on the Sense of Existence. Munich: Wilhelm Goldmann.

Uwe C. Schöne. 2007. The Bible of the 21st Century. Knowledge instead of Faith. Understanding God's Universe. Norderstedt: BoD – Books on Demand.

Scientific summaries in videos and YouTube posts:

Expert Discovers Jesus' Death Certificate

Shroud of Turin Secrets that Continue to Baffle Scientists

TURIN SHROUD Images REVEAL Words 'THE LAMB' Written on Object under the Beard

2018 UPDATE! SHROUD OF TURIN REVEALS SECRETS STRANGE END TIMES SIGNS

Scientists "Jesus Rose from The Dead!" Astounding Proof!

Proof that the Shroud of Turin is the Burial Cloth of Jesus Christ!

Shroud of Turin ~ Amazing Proof of the Resurrection of Jesus.

Part 2 Science Explains Shroud Image NEW 2016 Video

Science Explains Shroud Image! 2016 BEST NEW VIDEO!

The Most Comprehensive Presentation on the Shroud on YouTube 4

Shroud of Turin! HD 720p

Documented Evidence of Jesus' Resurrection

Zeitfracht Medien GmbH
Ferdinand-Jühlke-Straße 7
99095 Erfurt, Deutschland
produktsicherheit@kolibri360.de